AN ISRAELITE PERSPECTIVE ON RACE AND COLOR

Concerning Kush, Kushite, Black and Black Skin

NOVEMBER 19, 2022

OHR BAYIT

CONCERNING BLACK, KUSHITE, AND BLACK SKIN

Contents

Mishnah Negaim 2:1 3

Chizkuni, Genesis 8:18 3

Aramiac Targum to Lamentations 5 4

Bekhorot 44b:17 4

Bekhorot 45b 4

Rashi on Song of Songs 1:5 5

Sanhedrin 108b:15 6

Berakhot 58b 6

Ibn Ezra on Numbers 12:1 7

Zephaniah 1:1 8

Rashi on Numbers 12:1:3 8

Rashi on Numbers 12:1 8

Misneh Torah Blessings 10 8

Rashi on Numbers 12:1 9

Jeremiah 13:23 9

Moed Katan 16b:18 9

Midrash Tanchuma, Tzav 13:1 10

Onkelos Numbers 12:1 10

Pirkei DeRabbi Eliezer 53:6 10

Rashi on Psalms 7:1:2 11

Radak on Psalms 7:1:2 11

Zephaniah 1 11

Kabbalah 12

Zohar 1:15a:1 13

Zohar 1:51a:2 13

Zohar 1:51a:4 13

Zohar 3:47b:10 13

Shaarei Kedusha, Part 1 1:5 13

Zohar 1:12a:8 14

Zohar 1:16a:9 14

Shaarei Kedusha, Part 1 2:7 14

Zohar 1:51a:10 14

Zohar 1:77b:8 14

Zohar 1:51a:3 15

Tikkunei Zohar 145a:4 15

Zohar 9Or Neerav, PART VI 4:4 15

Zohar 1:51a:8 15

Zohar 9 13:208 16

Nimrod **17**

Review 18

Mishnah Negaim 2:1

1.   **Rabbi Ishmael says: the children of Israel (may I be atonement for them!) are like boxwood[1], neither black nor white but of an intermediate shade.** Rabbi Ishmael says that we use the skin of Israelites, which is dark but not black, as the barometer. This is because the laws of negaim were stated with regard to Israelites. As an aside, Rabbi Ishmael offers to take upon himself vicarious atonement for Israel's sins.

Chizkuni, Genesis 8:18

1.   I, "Noach and his sons left the ark, etc." Some commentators claim that although marital relations between the sexes had been permitted again, the manner in which the Torah writes the males exiting from the ark as if in a group is revealing. On the other hand, the Talmud in Sanhedrin 108 states that there were three creatures which violated the prohibition of sexual relations during their stay in the ark: the dog, the raven and Noach's son Cham. All of them were punished for their misconduct. The dog is tied by a chain or leash to its owner. The raven is forced to spit after indulging in mating, and Cham's skin, or that of his offspring, turns black.

---

[1] The Israelites are described as neither black of white but intermediate and dark but not black. Based upon these statements, we can conclude that the Israelites had skin of a brown color. Box woods resemble this description. Boxwood is Daniel 10:6. The book of Daniel describes a man dressed in linen whose arms and legs had color of burnished bronze.

Aramiac Targum to Lamentations 5

1. Our skin has become black like an oven, because of the exhaustion of starvation.

Bekhorot 44b:17

1. The Gemara asks: But if so, **this is** identical to one whose skin is extremely **black,** and the Mishnah on 45b explicitly states that such a priest is disqualified from performing the Temple service. The Gemara responds: Rabbi Ḥanina ben Antigonus learns from the Mishna only that a *mero'aḥ ashekh* is disqualified; he **does not teach** in that Mishna the *halakha* that a person with extremely **black** skin is blemished.

Bekhorot 45b

1. GEMARA: The Mishna teaches that a kushi, a giḥor, and a lavkan are disqualified. The Gemara explains: A kushi is one whose skin is extremely black, a giḥor is one whose skin is extremely white, and a lavkan is one whose skin is extremely red. The Gemara asks: Is that so? But there was a certain person who said to others: Who wants a lukiyani lamb, and the lamb was found to be white. Rather, a kushi is one whose skin is extremely black; a giḥor is one whose skin is extremely red, as people say about one whose skin is extremely red: Giḥia red; and a lavkan is one whose skin is extremely white, as in the case of that person who said: Who wants a lukiyani, and it was found to be white.

Rashi on Song of Songs 1:5

1. I am Black but comely, etc. You, my friends, let me not be light in your eyes. Even if my husband has left me because of my blackness, for I am Black because of the tanning of the sun, but I am comely with the shape of beautiful limbs. Though I am Black like the tents of Keidar, which are blackened because of the rains, for they are always spread out in the wilderness, I am easily cleansed to become like the curtains of Shlomo. ***The allegory is: The congregation of Yisroel says to the nations, "I am Black in my deeds [i.e., sins], but I am comely by virtue of the deeds of my ancestors, and even some of my deeds are comely.*** If I bear the iniquity of the [golden] calf,20 I can offset it with the merit of the acceptance of the Torah." [Scripture] calls the nations, "the daughters בָּנוֹת of Yerusholayim" because it is destined to become the metropolis for them all, as Yechezkeil prophesied, "I will give them to you as surrounding villages 21",לִבְנוֹת and similarly, "Ekron, and its suburbs 22".וּבְנֹתֶיהָ

2. **Rashi on Song of Songs 1:5:1**

    a. If I bear the iniquity of the [golden] calf,20According to Targum the faces of the Bnei Yisroel actually turned black like the skin of the Cushites, when they sinned with the golden calf.

CONCERNING BLACK, KUSHITE, AND BLACK SKIN

Sanhedrin 108b:15

1. The Sages taught: Three violated that directive and engaged in intercourse while in the ark, and all of them were punished for doing so. They are: The dog, and the raven, and Ham, son of Noah. The dog was punished in that it is bound; the raven was punished in that it spits, and Ham was afflicted in that his skin turned black.

Berakhot 58b

1. The Gemara continues to discuss the obligation to recite a blessing over unusual phenomena. Rabbi Yehoshua ben Levi said: One who sees spotted people recites: Blessed…Who makes creatures different. The Gemara raises a challenge: One who saw a person with unusually Black skin, a person with unusually red skin, a person with unusually white skin [lavkan], an unusually tall and thin person, a dwarf, or one with warts [darnikos]recites: Blessed…Who makes creatures different. However, one who sees an amputee, a blind person, a flat-headed person, a lame person, one afflicted with boils, or spotted people recites: Blessed…the true Judge, not: Who makes creatures different.

Ibn Ezra on Numbers 12:1

1. Now va-tedabber is in the feminine. Thus, our verse is to be rendered, And Miriam spoke, and Aaron. If both spoke, then our text should have read, va-yedabberu miriam ve-aharon. Hence, he was also punished. Va-tedabber (spoke) is followed by a bet2 and has a negative connotation. It is similar to va-yedabber ha-am be-Elohim (And the people spoke against God) (Num. 21:5). The verb dabber (spoke) followed by a bet is also found with a positive connotation.3 It also appears in prophetic statements.4 Some say that Moses was king of Cush5 and took a Cushite woman. ***6 Onkelos renders Cushite beautiful.7 According to Onkelos, Cushite is an honorific term.*** The Arabs similarly call pitch white. We too refer to a blind person by the term sege nahor (rich of light).8 But it is illogical9 to turn a positive name into a negative one.10 Some say that Cush the Benjaminite (Ps. 7:1) refers to Saul.11 They say the same with regard to Are ye not as the children of the Ethiopians (Khushiyyim) unto Me (Amos 9:7).12 I have already explained this.13I believe that the Cushite woman is to be identified with Zipporah, for Zipporah was a Midianite.14 The Midianites are Ishmaelites15 and they live in tents.16 Scripture similarly writes: The curtains17 of the land of Midian do tremble (Hab. 3:7). Because of the sun18 they do not have any whiteness at all. Zipporah was black and was like a Cushite.

CONCERNING BLACK, KUSHITE, AND BLACK SKIN

Zephaniah 1:1

1. The word of the LORD that came to Zephaniah son of Cushi son of Gedaliah son of Amariah's son of Hezekiah, during the reign of King Josiah's son of Amon of Judah.

Rashi on Numbers 12:1:3

1. THE CUSHITE WOMAN — This tells us that all agreed as to her beauty just as all agree as to the blackness of an Aethopian (cf. Sifrei Bamidbar 99).

Rashi on Numbers 12:1

1. THE CUSHITE WOMAN — Because of her beauty-she was called, "the Aethiopian" just as a man calls his handsome son "Moor," in order that the evil eye should have no power over him (Midrash Tanchuma, Tzav 13).

Misneh Torah Blessings 10

1. On seeing a Cushite [Rabbinic euphemism for a person of color], or anyone unusual in facial appearance or conformation of his limbs, one says, "Blessed art Thou, O Lord our God, King of the Universe, Who variest the forms of creatures." On seeing a blind person, a person with a physical disability, or one afflicted with boils or tetters, etc. the blessing said is "Blessed art Thou, O Lord our God, King of the Universe, the true Judge." If the affliction is congenital, the blessing is "Who variest the forms of creatures." On seeing an elephant, an

ape, or an owl one says, "Blessed be He Who varieth the forms of creatures."

Rashi on Numbers 12:1

1. Cushite. [כּוּשִׁית is] numerically equivalent to יְפַת מַרְאֶה, ("beautiful in appearance.")

Jeremiah 13:23

1. Can the Cushite change his skin, Or the leopard his spots? Just as much can you do good, who are practiced in doing evil!

Moed Katan 16b:18

1. The response to this admonishment is found in the verse, as it is written: "Shiggaion of David, which he sang to the Lord, concerning the words of Cush the Benjaminite" (Psalms 7:1). Is Cush his name? Saul is his name. Rather, this is a designation that indicates: Just as a Cushite, a native of the ancient kingdom of Cush in eastern Africa, is distinguished by his dark skin, so too, Saul was distinguished by his actions, as he was absolutely righteous and performed many good deeds. Therefore, David uses the word shiggaion as an allusion to the error [shegia] that he had made when he sang a song of praise over Saul's downfall.

Midrash Tanchuma, Tzav 13:1

2. As he took a Cushite woman" - the numerical value of Cushite is [equal to that of] beautiful looks. The tally of this one is like the tally for that one...."The Cushite woman" tells [us] that everybody concedes about her beauty, in the same way as everyone speaks about the blackness of a Cushite...."As he took a Cushite woman" - what do we learn to say [from here]?...And she is called a Cushite because of her pleasantness; in the same way as a man will call his pleasant son, Cushite, so that the [evil] eye not [come to] overpower him.

Onkelos Numbers 12:1

1. Miriam and Aharon spoke about Moshe concerning the Cushite [fair] woman that he married, for, he married [sent away] a Cushite [fair] woman.

Pirkei DeRabbi Eliezer 53:6

1. Just as the body of this Cushite is different from all creatures, so do the Israelites differ from all the nations of the world in their ways and by their good deeds; therefore, are they called Cushites...One Scripture saith, "And Ebedmelech, the Cushite, said." Was it Ebed? Was he not Baruch, son of Neriah? But just as this Cushite is different in his body from all other people, so was Baruch, son of Neriah, different in his deeds and good ways from the rest of the sons of men.... Therefore, he was called a Cushite.

Rashi on Psalms 7:1:2

1. Cush Just as a Cushite has unusual skin, so did Saul have unusual deeds.

Radak on Psalms 7:1:2

1. And he calls him Cush because he was beautiful, as "the Cushite woman" , which is interpreted in the Targum as "the beautiful woman"; and such is the opinion of all the exegetes....And they say that he calls him "Cushite" as a Cushite is one who does not change his skin, so Saul did not change in his hatred towards David....And in this way it is said , "Can the Cushite change his skin or the leopard his spots? Then may ye also be able to do good who are accustomed to evil." And the learned R.

Zephaniah 1

1. The word of the LORD that came to Zephaniah son of Cushi son of Gedaliah son of Amariah's son of Hezekiah, during the reign of King Josiah's son of Amon of Judah.

Kabbalah

Perspective on black

CONCERNING BLACK, KUSHITE, AND BLACK SKIN

Zohar 1:15a:1

1. The spark was then inserted into the center of a circle that was neither white nor black nor red nor green, nor any color at all.

Zohar 1:51a:2

1. One white, shining light; and one light to which black or blue is attached. The white light is on top, and it rises in a straight path. And the blue or black light is beneath it, and it is a seat to the white.

Zohar 1:51a:4

1. At times, this blue-black changes to red, but the white light above it never changes, for it is constantly white.... However, the blue changes to these [other] colors; at times it is blue or black, and at times it is red. And it is attached on both sides.

Zohar 3:47b:10

1. Black. If it were not for black one would never know white, because Blackness causes whiteness to disappear and become more precious.

Shaarei Kedusha, Part 1 1:5

1. human body is fashioned from the good that is within four foundations - fire, wind, water, dust, their fashioning from the bad that is in them is fashioned from four biles which are - the white, the Black person.

CONCERNING BLACK, KUSHITE, AND BLACK SKIN

Zohar 1:12a:8

1. Black light within white light. Both are as one without separation.

Zohar 1:16a:9

1. Darkness is a black fire that is strong in color, because no other color can change black. It is also a red fire that is strong in its appearance, as red is the most noticeable color.

Shaarei Kedusha, Part 1 2:7

1. Just as there are four bodily elements composed of good and evil; the white, green, black, and red humors, and these powers either establish a physically healthy body or damage it, so is it regarding the

Zohar 1:51a:10

1. In the holy name YHVH,1The four letters of the name of God represent four stages of ever-increasing divine manifestation. the second letter hé is the blue or black light attached to the remaining letters

Zohar 1:77b:8

1. The secret is that the black flame does not hold on to the white flame before it is aroused. As soon as it is aroused first, the white flame immediately rests upon it.

Zohar 1:51a:3

1. The light that is either black or a shade of blue that is below, is a throne of glory to the white [light]. And herein lies the secret of techelet.... And this blue-black throne is attached to another object below it that kindles it and arouses it to attach itself to the white light.

Tikkunei Zohar 145a:4

1. Although Her pupil was black, through it and from it will the Holy One light up the world, for He will illuminate Her.

Zohar 9Or Neerav, PART VI 4:4

1. Black develops into dark blue. Some have interpreted that its color is that of the sapphire, which is the beginning of all colors and is near to the color blue.

Zohar 1:51a:8

1. And though it be in the nature of the blue or black light to destroy whatever it touches beneath, yet Israel, cleaving to it from beneath, are not destroyed; so it is said, "But ye that cleave unto the...Your God and not our God; that is to say, it is the blue or black flame, consuming and annihilating whatever cleaves to it from below, and still you cleave and are alive.

Zohar 9 13:208

1. One whose sign is a man incorporates from the good side every good trait, he is pious, wise mighty in Torah, fears sin, full of many good qualities and his face will be **_blackish._**

Nimrod

The Origin of Idolatry and Wickedness

Review

Judaism is replete with references to black, black skin, Kushi, Kushite, and seemingly negative expressions based solely upon the color of one's skin. However, when we look into the both the Written Torah and Oral Torah with an unbiased view a different reality becomes clear. Are we discussing race or character?

I would conclude based upon the provided texts, Torah, and Zohar, that the origins of the black conversations are rooted in Nimrod and his Evil character. As Bereshit states, "Nimrod was a mighty warrior and mighty hunter on Earth. He built a great city, and the people of the earth would say, "Like Nimrod a mighty hunter before Hashem". (Bereshit 10:6-13). Who was Nimrod? Son of Kush and son of Cham. (Bereshit 9:7-8).

Nimrod ruled the people and the earth through fear and might. He subjected the people to Avodah Zerah through manipulation and entice. Nimrod rebelled against Hashem by making himself God. He used the power of Garments the ruled the people and he proclaimed himself as a god. What were the garments? The garments of Adam. Bereshit 3:21, and Hashem made them garments of skin. Nimrod possessed the skins and wielded unchecked power upon the earth. The people of the earth would have loathed, despised, and hated Nimrod for the evils he committed against mankind, namely those who were righteous. Namely Israel. (Debarim 32:8.) From the righteous Noach leading up to our Holy Patriarch Abraham Avinu.

Abraham lived during the lifetime of Nimrod and was born and raised in the kingdom of Nimrod. (Bereshit 11:20-32). Abraham knew well and experienced firsthand Nimrod's wickedness and idolatry. Hashem told Abraham to get out of the land of his father's, meaning land of idolatry so that the truth of creation and the center of the world could be revealed to him. Abraham tried but could not reveal the governor of the land of Israel. When Hashem saw his dedication He said, get out so that I can show you a land (root of righteousness). Terach, Abraham's father fled taking Abraham and Sarah with him among others. Terach fled for fear of the people and Abraham fled for love and fear of Hashem.

Nimrod, son of Kush was the founder of Idolatry. He murdered and maimed men. He subjugated all of humanity for hundreds of years, namely the righoutues Israel and forced worship of himself as Elohim. It would be logical and natural for the predecessors of Israel and Abraham Avinu to know and teach the wickedness of Nimrod son of Kush to their descendants. This seeming racial topic is not related to race at all but a righteous decrying of evil and wickedness. What is Israel is consistent focus on Kush? It is the remembering of the wickedness he brought upon the earth. He Kush was the first man of might (tyrant) upon the earth. As we are commanded to remember and destroy Amalek (Shemot 17:8-16) so should we remember and eradicate the Avodah Zerah created and perpetuated by Nimrod and his descendants. It is not a matter of race but of Evil vs Good. Nimrod king of Kush favored and lived his life to perpetuate Evil.

Zohar 1:78b:4

Nevertheless, "And from the wicked their light is withheld" applies to Nimrod and the people of his generation, whom Abraham left, since he was "their light"; "the high arm shall be broken" alludes to...Nimrod.

Zohar 1:78b:5

And the high arm shall be broken" applies to Nimrod, who misled the whole world into following him.

Zohar 1:137b:4

Here it is written, "For he relished his venison," which is similar to, "wherefore it is said, 'like Nimrod the mighty hunter before Hashem'".

Zohar 1:142b:2

These are the garments Esau took from Nimrod....They are the precious garments from Adam, which came to the hands of Nimrod, who used them when he hunted, as it is written, "He was a mighty hunter before Hashem" .... And Esau went into the field, where he fought with and killed Nimrod, removing the garments from him. This is the meaning of ", and Esau came from the field, and he was faint" .... Here too, there is killing, because Esau murdered Nimrod.

Pesachim 118a:20

This Gemara elaborates: When the evil Nimrod threw our father, Abraham, into the fiery furnace, Gabriel said before the Holy One, Blessed be He: Master of the Universe, I will descend and cool the furnace

Avot D'Rabbi Natan 33:2

XV, 7ff. once in Ur of the Chaldees13According to a tradition, Abraham had been thrown by Nimrod into a fiery furnace because of his belief in God, from which he came forth unharmed.

Eruvin 53a:7

Rav and Shmuel both identified Amraphel with Nimrod. However, one said: Nimrod was his name. And why was his name called Amraphel...And why was his name called Nimrod? Because he caused the entire world to rebel [himrid] against God during his reign.

Chullin 89a:7

I granted greatness to Nimrod, yet he said: "Come, let us build a city and a tower, with its top in heaven, and let us make for ourselves a name".

Pesachim 94b:1

the disciple in corruption of Nimrod the wicked, who caused the entire world to rebel against Me during his reign by advising the generation of the dispersion to build a tower in order to fight the Hosts.

Avodah Zarah 53b:13

GEMARA: Rabbi Yirmeya bar Abba says that Rav says: The temple of Nimrod, i.e., the remnants of the tower of Babel, is considered a place of idol worship whose worshippers abandoned it in peacetime.

Tractate Soferim 21:9

Nimrod.70 Mentioned in Gen. 10, 8ff. Og went and built sixty cities, the smallest of which was sixty miles high, as it is stated, Threescore cities, all the region of Argob.71Deut. 3, 4.

Avodah Zarah 3a:8

Let Nimrod come and testify about Abraham that he did not engage in idol worship. Let Laban come and testify to Jacob that he is not suspected with regard to robbery.

Chagigah 13a:2

follower of the ways, of Nimrod the wicked, who caused the entire world to rebel against Him during the time of his reign.

Akeidat Yitzchak 44:4:5

Ever since Terach who had been subservient to Nimrod, Israel's forbears had always been dependent in some manner on other rulers.... When G-d discovered Abraham and removed him from the grasp of Nimrod, He did so by exercising His claim to the jewels found in Nimrod's kingdom.

Derashot HaRan 1:13

This, because they all subscribed to idol worship, and the valley, too, which they chose for themselves was the land of Shinar, who's chief and king was Nimrod, the high potentate of idolatry, who persecuted...For when Abraham fled Nimrod for Canaan, if Nimrod had ruled the entire universe, where would he flee from his wrath?

Derashot HaRan 1:12

So that the first to begin this call, Abraham, experienced what he did at the hands of Nimrod until he was compelled to leave his land and go to a different one.

Derekh Chayim 5:4:9

And know about these forefathers: Avraham's beginning was with pain, as he was pursued by Nimrod. But afterwards all of his days were with goodness and blessing.

English Explanation of Pirkei Avot 5:3:1

twice in connection with his two wives, once on the occasion of his war with the kings, once at the covenant between the pieces, once in Ur of the Chaldees, when he was thrown into a fire furnace by Nimrod

And this is his language: At first, Nimrod sought to kill him, and he hid in the ground for thirteen years; than they threw him into the fiery furnace in Ur Casdim; [God] exiled him from his birthplace.

Derekh Chayim 5:4:7

And just like the Holy One, blessed be He, took him out of Ur Kasdim after he was pursued by Nimrod; so [too] did the Holy One, blessed be He, take Israel out of Egypt.

Bartenura on Pirkei Avot 5:3:1

Ten tests: One - Ur Kasdim, when Nimrod cast him into the fiery furnace; the second - "'Go out from your land'"; the third - "and there was a famine"; the fourth - "and the woman was taken to the house

Rabbeinu Yonah on Pirkei Avot 5:3:1

With ten tests Abraham, our father, was tested - and he withstood them all: The first was 'Ur Kasdim' - that Nimrod dropped him down into the fiery furnace and he was saved.

Abram by observing his star at his birth; see infra, pp. 377 f.; and cf. Beer, Das Leben Abrahams, pp. 98 f.

Pirkei DeRabbi Eliezer 24:4

Rabbi Chakhinai said: Nimrod was a mighty hero, as it is said, "And Cush begat Nimrod, who began to be a mighty one in the earth" ...., blessed be He, made for Adam and his wife, were with Noah in the ark, and when they went forth from the ark, || Ham, the son of Noah, brought them forth with him, and gave them as an inheritance to Nimrod...The sons of men thought that this to the power of his might; therefore they made him king over themselves, as it is said, "Wherefore it is said, Like Nimrod, a mighty hunter before the Lord" .

Pirkei DeRabbi Eliezer 24:1

NIMROD AND THE TOWER OF BABEL Noah brought his sons and his grandsons, and he blessed them with their settlements, and he gave them as an inheritance all the earth.

Pirkei DeRabbi Eliezer 24:5

Nimrod said to his people: Come, let us build a great city for ourselves, and let us dwell therein, lest we be scattered upon the face of all the earth, as the first people.

Pirkei DeRabbi Eliezer 24:3

Rabbi 'Aḳiba said: They cast off the Kingdom of Heaven from themselves, and appointed Nimrod king over themselves; a slave son of a slave. Are not all the sons of Ham slaves?

Pirkei DeRabbi Eliezer 24:12

Rabbi Meir said: Esau, the brother of Jacob, saw the coats of Nimrod, and in his heart, he coveted them, and he slew him, and took them from him. Whence that they were desirable in his sight?

Shir HaShirim Rabbah 2:5:1

Alternatively, "support me with raisin cakes [ba'ashishot]," with many fires [ishot]; with the fire of Abraham,52This is a reference to the fiery furnace into which Nimrod cast Abraham; see Bereshit Rabba

Vayikra Rabbah 27:4

Abraham was pursued by Nimrod, and the Holy One chose Abraham. Isaac was pursued by the Philistines, and the Holy One chose Isaac. Jacob was pursued by Esau, and the Holy One chose Jacob.

CONCERNING BLACK, KUSHITE, AND BLACK SKIN

Pirkei DeRabbi Eliezer 27:1

Amraphel is identified with Nimrod in T.B. 'Erubin, 53a. See Gen. Rab. 42:4. came against him3 See Jalḵuṭ, Gen. § 68, which has used P.R.E. to slay him.4 See T.B. Synhedrin, 95b.

Shir HaShirim Rabbah 8:8:2

"What shall we do for our sister on the day that she will be spoken for" – on the day that the wicked Nimrod decreed and said that [Abraham] would be thrown into the fiery furnace.

Shir HaShirim Rabbah 8:9:3

When Assyria will come into our land, and when it will tread in our palaces, we shall raise against it seven shepherds…" .36. The next verse states that they will lay waste to Assyria and "the land of Nimrod.

Pirkei DeRabbi Eliezer 32:12

Esau went on the way of death, because he slew Nimrod and his son Chavir, and he almost sought to kill Jacob his brother, as it is said, "The days of mourning for my father are at hand, and I will slay.

Pirkei DeRabbi Eliezer 11:12

The second king was Nimrod, who ruled from one end of the world to the other, for all the creatures were dwelling in one place and they were afraid of the waters of the flood, and Nimrod was king over.

Midrash Tanchuma, Lech Lecha 6:3

Because he ordered Abraham: "Fall into the fiery furnace."10Amraphel is identified with Nimrod in many sources.

Otzar Midrashim, The Aleph Bet of ben Sira, The Alphabet of ben Sira, (alternative version) 33

There was once an unendingly beautiful horse belonging to Nimrod. The other horses said to him, 'Give us your head to cut off, and we will give you a house full of straw and barley.'

Sefer HaYashar (midrash), Book of Genesis, Toldot 4

And all the great men of Nimrod, who were out hunting with Nimrod in the wilderness, when they heard the terrible yelling recognized at once the voices of those two men, and they hastened to ascertain...And when Esau saw from a distance the mighty men of Nimrod coming towards him, he fled and escaped; and Esau took along with him the costly garments of Nimrod, bequeathed to Nimrod by his father, and...by virtue of which garments Nimrod prevailed over all the people of the earth; and Esau ran hastily and concealed those garments in his house....And when Nimrod, the son of Cush, was dead, his men took him up and carried him away midst great consternation, and they buried him in his city....Thus Nimrod died by the sword of Esau in shame and disgrace, and his death was caused by the seed of Abraham, as he himself foresaw it in his dreams.

Sefer HaYashar (midrash), Book of Genesis, Noach 13

And Nimrod, the king, reigned securely, and he was the sole
ruler of all the earth.... And all the earth was of one speech
and one language, and all the princes of Nimrod, as also
Phut, and Mizraim, and Cush, and Canaan, and all their
families together consulted at that time, and they

Pirkei DeRabbi Eliezer 16:13

When went forth from Ur of the Chaldees all the magnates of
the kingdom came to give him gifts; and Nimrod took his
first-born Eliezer and gave him to as a perpetual slave.

Sefer HaYashar (midrash), Book of Genesis, Noach 8

And then Nimrod placed officers over them, and took from
their children hostages for security, that all would be
servants unto him and unto his brothers....And after Nimrod
had thus reduced the people to servitude, he would return
home with his men....And after the conquests of Nimrod
increased and he always returned victoriously triumphant
from the battles with all their enemies around them, then
the people all united and came unto Nimrod and
elected...And Nimrod then appointed princes, and judges,
and generals over his people after the manner of kings, and
for his commander-in-chief Nimrod selected Terah the son of
Nahor, and he elevated him in greatness...And Nimrod called
the name of that city Shinar, for the Lord had discomfited all
his enemies before him, that he might conquer them.

Sefer HaYashar (midrash), Book of Genesis, Noach 9

And in the night that Abram was born, all the servants of Terah and all the wise men and the astrologers of Nimrod came, and they ate and drank in the house of Terah and they were greatly rejoiced.

Sefer HaYashar (midrash), Book of Genesis, Noach 18

Nimrod making his home in Babel, where he established the seat of his government for himself and all his officers....And Nimrod reigned securely once more, and his servants and princes gave unto Nimrod the additional name of Amraphel, saying: All his people and all his princes were dispersed through the building of...And for all those hardships Nimrod would not return unto the Lord, but he would only add new sins and transgressions to those already committed....And Mardon, the son of Nimrod, was if possible, more wicked than his father, committing yet worse outrages and abominations than his father, and leading the sons of man unto total depravity.

Midrash Tanchuma, V'Zot HaBerachah 6:1

Abraham experienced death, Nimrod experienced death; Isaac experienced death, Abimelech experienced death; Moses experienced death, Pharaoh experienced death; for Solomon has stated, "Everyone is going

Otzar Midrashim, Avraham our Father, The Story of Avraham our Father, and Nimrod 3

Nimrod was a heretic concerning the truth of the lord blessed be him. He was conceited and he said that he himself was a God. And the people of his time served and bowed to him.... And he [Nimrod] trembled with great fear. What did he do? He sent after his lesser officers, and he told them this matter.... When Nimrod heard their advice, he was greatly gladdened much so.... So commanded King Nimrod and they left the house with honor.

Sefer HaYashar (midrash), Book of Genesis, Noach 7

And Cush, the son of Ham, the son of Noah, took unto himself a wife at that time in his old age, and he began a son, and he called his name Nimrod, saying: At that time the sons of man again began to...But finally when Cush begat Nimrod, whom he loved above his other sons, Cush gave the garments unto Nimrod. And when Nimrod grew up and was twenty-one years of age, he put on those garments....And Nimrod was possessed of more strength than all his brothers....And at the time when Nimrod was forty years of age, there was a war between his brothers and the sons of Japheth, and his brethren were under the hand of their enemy....And Nimrod strengthened himself at that time, and went forth and assembled all the families of the sons of Cush, about four hundred and sixty men.

Midrash Tanchuma, Toldot 4:1

After Nimrod caused Abraham to be hurled into the fiery furnace, the Holy One, blessed be He, descended to rescue him.

2.

Sefer HaYashar (midrash), Book of Genesis, Noach 29

And in the tenth year of Abram's dwelling in the land a war raged between Nimrod king of Shinar, and Chedorlaomer king of Elam, and Nimrod came to do battle with Chedorlaomer and to humble him under...Therefore when Nimrod heard that the people of the plain revolted against Chedorlaomer, Nimrod hastened to make war against him, and he came full of pride and contempt....And Nimrod assembled all his princes and servants, about seven thousand men, and he went against Chedorlaomer....And all those kings engaged in battle in that place, and Nimrod and all his people were humbled before the men of Chedorlaomer, and there fell in that battle of Nimrod's men about six thousand....And Mardon the son of Nimrod was among the slain. And Nimrod fled and returned to his country in shame and contempt.

Sefer HaYashar (midrash), Book of Genesis, Noach 10

It is but last night that, Lyon, the son of Nimrod, came into my house saying: Let me have thy beautiful horse which the king hath given unto thee, and I will give thee its full value in gold.

CONCERNING BLACK, KUSHITE, AND BLACK SKIN

Midrash Tanchuma, Lech Lecha 12:1

The wicked earneth false wages refers to the evil Nimrod, who erected idols and led mankind astray.

Legends of the Jews 1:6:21

After slaying Nimrod, Esau hastened cityward in great fear of his victim's followers. Tired and exhausted he arrived home to find Jacob busy preparing a dish of lentils.

Sefer HaYashar (midrash), Introduction 12

Second, we learn all about the birth of Abraham, and how his conversion to the Lord was brought about, and the events that transpired between him and Nimrod, also the occurrences of the confusion of tongues

Sefer HaYashar (midrash), Book of Genesis, Toldot 3

And Nimrod, king of Babel, whose name was Amraphel, went likewise very frequently with his great men to hunt in the field, and to walk about with them in the cool of the day....And Nimrod kept close watch concerning Esau, for Nimrod's heart was filled with jealousy against Esau all the time...., but they separated from him going into the distance to hunt in different directions, and Esau had hidden himself lying in wait for Nimrod in the wilderness. ...And Nimrod and his men with him knew nothing of Esau and they strolled to and from in the field at the cool of day, to ascertain whither his men had gone to hunt in the field.... And when Nimrod with his two men came near to the hiding place, Esau suddenly jumped towards them from his ambuscade, and drawing his sword he ran to Nimrod and cut off his head.

Midrash Tanchuma, Achrei Mot 1:1

This refers to Nimrod, who incited all the whole world against the Holy One, blessed be He. The former is dead, and the latter is dead. "To the good, to the clean, and to the unclean."

Legends of the Jews 1:5:22

Abraham: "Yes, mother, the God of the heavens and the God of the earth, He is also the God of Nimrod son of Canaan. Go, therefore, and carry this message unto Nimrod."

Sefer HaYashar (midrash), Book of Genesis, Noach 27

came secretly to visit his son Abram in the house of Noah, and Terah stood still very high in the eyes of the king and in the eyes of the people, And Abram said unto his father: Knowest thou not that Nimrod...Haran—In Canaan—Nimrod vanquished—Rikayon the first Pharaoh—His great cunning—How he accumulated wealth—Famine in Canaan—Abram removes to Egypt—He smuggles Sarai across the river in a box.

Legends of the Jews 1:5:60

Indeed, it had been his fault that Abraham came near losing his life at the hands of Nimrod.

Legends of the Jews 1:5:46

Then the mother of Abraham came to him and implored him to pay homage to Nimrod and escape the impending misfortune.... When his mother heard these words, she spake, "May the God whom thou serves rescue thee from the fire of Nimrod!"

Kohelet Rabbah 3:15:1

Abraham was pursued by Nimrod, and the Holy One blessed be He chose Abraham, as it is stated: "You are the Lord God who chose Abram".

Legends of the Jews 1:5:21

The mother: "My son, is there a God beside Nimrod?"

Legends of the Jews 1:5:35

Serve the God of all gods," returned Abraham, "the Lord of lords, who hath created heaven and earth, the sea and all therein--the God of Nimrod and the God of Terah, the God of the east, the west, the...Who is Nimrod, the dog, who calleth himself a god, that worship be offered unto him?"

Legends of the Jews 1:5:27

Now Abraham, at the command of God, was ordered by the angel Gabriel to follow Nimrod to Babylon....was in no wise equipped to undertake a campaign against the king, but Gabriel calmed him with the words: "Thou needs no provision for the way, no horse to ride upon, no warriors to carry on war with Nimrod.

Ein Yaakov (Glick Edition), Avodah Zarah 1:3

Nimrod may testify that Abraham did not worship idols. Laban may testify that Jacob was not suspected of robbery. The wife of Potiphar may testify that Joseph was not guilty of adultery.

Legends of the Jews 1:5:57

When Terah visited his son in his hiding-place, Abraham proposed that they leave the land and take up their abode in Canaan, in order to escape the pursuit of Nimrod....He said: "Consider that it was not for thy sake that Nimrod overloaded thee with honors, but for his own profit.

Legends of the Jews 1:4:99

The iniquity and godlessness of Nimrod reached their climax in the building of the Tower of Babel....His counsellors had proposed the plan of erecting such a tower, Nimrod had agreed to it, and it was executed in Shinar by a mob of six hundred thousand men.

Sefer HaYashar (midrash), Book of Genesis, Noach 17

And Nimrod, the son of Cush, was still in the land of Shinar and he ruled over it, and he dwelt therein, and he built many cities in the land of Shinar. ...And after Nimrod had built those cities in the land of Shinar, he, and the rest of his people, with their princes and heroes, dwelt in them,

Legends of the Jews 1:5:31

While Abraham proclaimed this with a loud voice, the idols fell upon their faces, and with them also King Nimrod....Thereupon Nimrod said, "Verily, the God of Abraham is a great and powerful God, the King of all kings," and he commanded Terah to take his son and remove him, and return again unto his own city, and father

Legends of the Jews 1:5:55

At the expiration of two years, it happened that Nimrod dreamed a dream. In his dream he found himself with his army near the fiery furnace in the valley into which Abraham had been cast.... When Nimrod examined his companions, he observed that they wore royal attire, and in form and stature they resembled himself.

Legends of the Jews 1:5:38

Nevertheless, great fear and terror took possession of Nimrod, because the people became more and more attached to the teachings of Abraham, and he knew not how to deal with the man who was undermining...Through his father Terah, Nimrod invited Abraham to come before him, that he might have the opportunity of seeing his greatness and wealth, and the glory of his dominion, and the multitude of his princes.

Midrash Tanchuma, Vayeshev 1:3

When He came to the genealogy of the sons of Ham, He said: The sons of Ham: Cush, and Mizraim ... and Cush begot Nimrod; thus, He indicated that they had become defiant, as it is said: He began to be mighty

Legends of the Jews 1:5:62

Terah had been a high official at the court of Nimrod, and he was held in great consideration by the king and his suite.... In the night of Abraham's birth, the astrologers and the wise men of Nimrod came to the house of Terah, and ate and drank, and rejoiced with him that night.

Legends of the Jews 1:5:161

Abraham: "I have taken upon me to speak unto the Lord, I who would have been turned long since into dust of the ground by Amraphel and into ashes by Nimrod, had it not been for Thy grace.

Legends of the Jews 1:5:30

Terah thereupon went to Nimrod and reported to him that his son Abraham had suddenly appeared in Babylon. The king sent for Abraham, and he came before him with his father.... Abraham passed the magnates and the dignitaries until he reached the royal throne, upon which he seized hold, shaking it and crying out with a loud voice: "O Nimrod, thou contemptible wretch, that denies

Legends of the Jews 1:5:45

Nimrod, however, was not to be turned aside from his purpose, to make Abraham suffer death by fire. One of the princes was dispatched to fetch him forth.... At that moment Satan, still disguised in human shape, approached Abraham, and said, "If thou desires' to deliver thyself from the fire of Nimrod, bow down before him and believe in him."

Legends of the Jews 1:5:24

Nimrod said, "Raise thy head and state thy request." Satan asked the king: "Why art thou terrified, and why are ye all in fear on account of a little lad?

Legends of the Jews 1:5:29

Therefore, Abraham spake to them, and said: "Ye serve a man of your own kind, and you pay worship to an image of Nimrod.

Legends of the Jews 1:5:5

His birth had been read in the stars by Nimrod, for this impious king was a cunning astrologer, and it was manifest to him that a man would be born in his day who would rise up against him and triumphantly

Legends of the Jews 1:5:23

Nimrod gave permission to Terah to rise and stated his request. Thereupon Terah related all that had happened with his wife and his son.... When Nimrod heard his tale, abject fear seized upon him, and he asked his counsellors and princes what to do with the lad. They answered and said: "Our king and our god!

Legends of the Jews 1:5:6

Then the angels appeared before God, and spoke, "Seest Thou not what he doth, yon sinner and blasphemer, Nimrod son of Canaarl, who slays so many innocent babes that have done no harm?"

Legends of the Jews 1:5:44

When the hangman raised his sword and set it at his throat to kill him, he exclaimed, "The Eternal He is God, the God of the whole world as well as of the blasphemer Nimrod."

Legends of the Jews 1:5:9

His mother lamented and said to her son: "Alas that I bore thee at a time when Nimrod is king.

Legends of the Jews 1:5:28

He is the God of the heavens, and the God of the gods, and the God of Nimrod. Acknowledge this as the truth, all ye men, women, and children.

Legends of the Jews 1:5:42

At the end of a year, the magnates of the realm presented themselves before the king, and advised him to cast Abraham into the fire, that the people might believe in Nimrod forever....The warden reminded the king that Abraham had not had food or drink a whole year, and therefore must be dead, but Nimrod nevertheless desired him to step in front of the prison and call his name.

Sefer HaYashar (midrash), Book of Genesis, Noach 21

And Nimrod dispatched three of his servants and they went and seized Abram and they brought him before the king.

Legends of the Jews 1:5:49

Abraham was the superior, not only of the impious king Nimrod and his attendants, but also of the pious men of his time, Noah, Shem, Eber, and Asshur.

Legends of the Jews 1:5:56

Nimrod took Anoko's words to heart and dispatched some of his servants to seize Abraham and kill him.... It happened that Eliezer, the slave whom Abraham had received as a present from Nimrod, was at that time at the royal court.

Legends of the Jews 1:4:94

The first among the leaders of the corrupt men was Nimrod....His father Cush had married his mother at an advanced age, and Nimrod, the offspring of this belated union, was particularly dear to him as the son of his old age.... When his son Nimrod reached his twentieth year, he gave them to him. These garments had a wonderful property. He who wore them was both invincible and irresistible.... The beasts and birds of the woods fell down before Nimrod as soon as they caught sight of him arrayed in them, and he was equally victorious in his combats with men.... This was done after a conflict between the descendants of Cush and the descendants of Japheth, from which Nimrod emerged triumphant, having routed the enemy utterly with the assistance of a handful.

Legends of the Jews 1:5:112

For one of the five, Amraphel, was none other than Nimrod, Abraham's enemy from of old.... Making the most of Chedorlaomer's embarrassment, Nimrod led a host of seven thousand warriors against his former general.... In the battle fought between Elam and Shinar, Nimrod suffered a disastrous defeat, he lost six hundred of his army, and among the slain was the king's son Mardon.

Legends of the Jews 1:5:43

and Abraham replied: "Food and drink have been bestowed upon me by Him who is over all things, the God of all gods and the Lord of all lords, who alone doeth wonders, He who is the God of Nimrod.

Legends of the Jews 1:5:25

Dismayed by the heavy clouds, they fled, returning to Nimrod, their king, and they said to him, "Let us depart and leave this realm," and the king gave money unto all his princes and his servants.

Legends of the Jews 1:5:7

If that be so, it behooves us not to violate the command of our god Nimrod." When he passed his hand over her body, there happened a miracle.

Midrash Tanchuma Buber, Toldot 3:1

Abraham has died, and Nimrod has died. SO, WHAT IS THE USE OF THIS BIRTHRIGHT TO ME? What was he cooking?

Legends of the Jews 1:5:48

But the princes of Nimrod interposed all with one voice, "Nay, our lord, this is not witchcraft, it is the power of the great God, the God of Abraham, beside whom there is no other god, and we acknowledge

Legends of the Jews 1:5:80

Terah hastened to Nimrod, bowed down before him, and besought him to hear his story, about his son who had been born to him fifty years back, and how he had done to his gods, and how he had spoken.

Legends of the Jews 1:5:59

Abraham told them all that had happened between Nimrod and himself, how he had been ready to be burnt for the glory of God, and how the Lord had rescued him from the flames.

Sefer HaYashar (midrash), Book of Genesis, Noach 26

And when Nimrod heard the words of Anuki, he sent his servants secretly to seize Abram and to bring him before the king to be slain.

Midrash Tanchuma Buber, Lech Lecha 2:1

In that, when Nimrod cast him into the midst of the fiery furnace,6Gen. R. 38:13; 39:3; 44:13; Cant. R. 8:8:2; Tanh., Gen. 3: 2....The ministering angels said to the Holy One: Sovereign of the World, behold, Nimrod has cast Abraham into the midst of the fiery furnace! R. Eliezer haQappar said: WE HAVE A LITTLE SISTER....On the day that Nimrod said to throw him into the midst of the fiery furnace, the Holy One said to the ministering angels: IF SHE IS A WALL, WE SHALL BUILD UPON HER A SILVER TURRET.

Midrash Tanchuma Buber, Vayera 2:1

WHO SLAYS A HUMAN < refers to > the one who killed Nimrod, < and > Nimrod is Amraphel .11Targum Ps. Joh. to Gen. 14:1; 'Eruv. 53a; Gen. R. 42:4; Tanh., Gen. 3:6; also, PRK 8:2; PR 18:3.

Sefer HaYashar (midrash), Book of Genesis, Vayishlach 14

Behold he delivered Abraham the Hebrew, their father, from the hands of Nimrod and all his people, who sought to slay him time and again; and from the fire, whereunto Nimrod had him cast, his God hath

Legends of the Jews 1:4:96

Men no longer trusted in God, but rather in their own prowess and ability, an attitude to which Nimrod tried to convert the whole world.... Therefore, people said, "Since the creation of the world there has been none like Nimrod, a mighty hunter of men and beasts, and a sinner before God."

Legends of the Jews 2:4:185

Nasargiel explained: "These are the sinners who committed incest, murder, and idolatry, who cursed their parents and their teachers, and who, like Nimrod and others, called themselves gods."

Midrash Tanchuma, Lech Lecha 2:1

It refers to Abraham at the time when Nimrod ordered that he be hurled into the fiery furnace. He was little because the Holy One, blessed be He, had not yet performed any miracles in his behalf.

Legends of the Jews 2:4:72

Surely, thou knowest that Abraham their father acted thus, who made the armies of Nimrod king of Babel and of Abimelech king of Gerar to stumble, and he possessed himself of the land of the children of Shinar.

Legends of the Jews 1:4:95

Since the flood there had been no such sinner as Nimrod. He fashioned idols of wood and stone, and paid worship to them.

Sefer HaYashar (midrash), Book of Genesis, Vayishlach 11

For such a thing hath never occurred since the days of Nimrod, nor in any of the former days hath such a thing come to pass.

Midrash Tanchuma Buber, Chukat 1:5

The Holy one said: O you wicked son of wickedness, son of Nimrod the Wicked, I am sending against you a tiny creature, the least of my creatures, to eradicate you from the world.

Legends of the Jews 1:6:19

The men slain by Esau on this day were Nimrod and two of his adjutants.... A long-standing feud had existed between Esau and Nimrod because the mighty hunter before the Lord was jealous of Esau, who also devoted himself assiduously to the chase.... Once when he was hunting it happened that Nimrod was separated from his people, only two men were with him. Esau, who lay in ambush, noticed his isolation, and waited until he should pass his covert....Then he threw himself upon Nimrod suddenly, and felled him and his two companions, who hastened to his succor....The outcries of the latter brought the attendants of Nimrod to the spot where he lay dead, but not before Esau had stripped him of his garments, and fled to the city with them.

Legends of the Jews 1:6:20

These garments of Nimrod had an extraordinary effect upon cattle, beasts, and birds. Of their own accord they would come and prostrate themselves before him who was arrayed in them.... Thus, Nimrod and Esau after him were able to rule over men and beasts.

Legends of the Jews 2:1:387

They had belonged to Nimrod. Once when the mighty hunter caught Esau in his preserves, and forbade him to go on the chase, they agreed to determine by combat what their privileges were.... Esau had taken counsel with Jacob, and he had advised him never to fight with Nimrod while he was clothed in Adam's garments.... The two now wrestled with each other, and at the time Nimrod was not dressed in Adam's clothes. The end was that he was slain by Esau.

Midrash Tanchuma, Emor 9:1

Abraham was pursued by Nimrod; and it is written "You are the Lord, the God who chose Abraham [...]."

Legends of the Jews 1:4:91

While Noah was still alive, the descendants of Shem, Ham, and Japheth appointed princes over each of the three groups- Nimrod for the descendants of Ham, Joktan for the descendants of Shem, and Phenech...Nimrod and Phenech flew into such a passion over the twelve men that they resolved to throw them into the fire.

Legends of the Jews 1:6:227

Jashub wondered thereat, for the like had not been heard from the days of Nimrod, and not even from the remotest times, that two men should be able to destroy so large a city, and he decided to go to war.

Sefer HaYashar (midrash), Book of Genesis, Lech Lecha 7

At that time Chedorlaomer, king of Elam, sent to all the kings around him, to Nimrod king of Shinor who was subjected to him in those days, and to Tidal king of Goyim, and to Arioch king of Ellasar with

Legends of the Jews 1:6:96

His grandfather had fled from Nimrod, and his father had gone away from the Philistines.

Midrash Tanchuma, Lech Lecha 2:2

What shall we do for our sister on the day that she shall be spoken for alludes to the day in which Nimrod ordered him hurled into the fiery furnace.

Sefer HaYashar (midrash), Book of Genesis, Vayishlach 12

For such a thing hath never occurred since the days of Nimrod, nor in any of the former days hath such a thing come to pass.

Legends of the Jews 3:5:101

In his youth Og had been a slave to Abraham, who had received him as a gift from Nimrod, for Og is none other than Eliezer, Abraham's steward.

CONCERNING BLACK, KUSHITE, AND BLACK SKIN

Legends of the Jews 4:2:5

under Mount Shechem, the seven golden idols called by the Amorites the holy nymphs the same seven idols which had been made in a miraculous way after the deluge by the seven sinners, Canaan, Put, Shelah, Nimrod.

Midrash Tanchuma Buber, Emor 12:2

Abraham was persecuted by Nimrod; YOU ARE THE LORD, THE GOD WHO CHOSE ABRAHAM. Isaac was persecuted by Philistines; AND THEY SAID: WE SEE PLAINLY < THAT THE LORD HAS BEEN WITH YOU >.

Ein Yaakov (Glick Edition), Chullin 6:4

The other nations, however, behave differently; for when I gave dignity unto Nimrod, he then said Come, let us build us a city. Unto Pharaoh, and he said Who is the Lord?

Legends of the Jews 4:10:95

A heavenly voice resounded: "O thou wicked man, son of a wicked man, and descendant of Nimrod the wicked, who incited the world to rebel against God!

Midrash Tanchuma Buber, V'Zot HaBerachah 5:1

Abraham experienced death; the wicked Nimrod experienced death; Isaac experienced death; Abimelech experienced death; Moses experienced death; the wicked Pharaoh experienced death; for Solomon has stated.

CONCERNING BLACK, KUSHITE, AND BLACK SKIN

Midrash Tanchuma Buber, Achrei Mot 1:1

This refers to Nimrod, who incited all the whole world against the Holy One. The former is dead, and the latter is dead. TO THE GOOD, TO THE CLEAN, [AND TO THE UNCLEAN.

Midrash Tanchuma Buber, Vayetzei 5:1

Abraham gave way to the hour and fled from Nimrod, the king of the Chaldeans. So, the hour returned and fell into his hand when he killed sixteen kings.

Sefer HaYashar (midrash), Book of Exodus 26

And verily, thou knowest that Abraham their father acted in like manner to deceive the hosts of Nimrod, king of Babel, and of Abimelech, king of Gerar, and that he appropriated the land of the children.

Ein Yaakov (Glick Edition), Pesakhim 10:17

for at the time when Nimrod, the wicked, had cast Abraham, our patriarch, into the fiery furnace, Gabriel said unto the Holy One, praised be He!

Kohelet Rabbah 2:14:1

Alternatively: "The wise man, his eyes are in his head" – this is Abraham our patriarch; "but the fool walks in darkness" – this is Nimrod; "I also know that one event will happen to them all."44.

Kohelet Rabbah 2:15:1

A midrash asserts that after Abraham defeated the four kings in battle, the surrounding nations referred to Abraham as their king. and the wicked Nimrod is called king.... Do the nations of the world say: Remember the action of Nimrod? That is what is written: "How can the wise man die like the fool?"

Kohelet Rabbah 4:14:1

kingship of the good inclination comes the beginning of the impoverishment of the evil inclination. Another matter: "Better is a poor...child" – this is Abraham; "than an old and foolish king" – this is Nimrod

Kohelet Rabbah 2:26:1

"But to the sinner He gave the task to gather and to amass" – this is Nimrod. And of whom is it stated: "To give to one who is good before God"?

Midrash Tanchuma Buber, Toldot 5:1

gt; from his execution by Nimrod. TO KEEP THEM ALIVE IN THE FAMINE, the one which came in his days, as stated: NOW THERE WAS A FAMINE IN THE LAND.

Midrash Tanchuma Buber, Lech Lecha 15:1

This refers to Nimrod the Wicked, who used to make images and lead astray the children of Adam; for idolatry resembles falsehood, as stated: FOR HIS MOLTEN IMAGE IS FALSEHOOD AND THERE IS NO BREATH INLegends of the Jews 2:2:66

Legends of the Jews 2:2:66

Then spake Nimrod the wicked, 'In my eyes there is none greater than he that taught me the language of Cush.' Together nations also answered in words like these, each one designated its angel.

www.ingramcontent.com/pod-product-compliance
Lightning Source LLC
Chambersburg PA
CBHW060916130726
48001CB00006B/2273